EMMANUEL JOSEPH

From Fast Fashion to Forever, Ecology and Ethics in the Clothing Industry

Copyright © 2025 by Emmanuel Joseph

All rights reserved. No part of this publication may be reproduced, stored or transmitted in any form or by any means, electronic, mechanical, photocopying, recording, scanning, or otherwise without written permission from the publisher. It is illegal to copy this book, post it to a website, or distribute it by any other means without permission.

First edition

This book was professionally typeset on Reedsy. Find out more at reedsy.com

Contents

1. Chapter 1: The Glitter and Gloom of Fast Fashion — 1
2. Chapter 2: The Hidden Cost of Cheap Clothes — 3
3. Chapter 3: The Environmental Footprint of Fast Fashion — 5
4. Chapter 4: The Human Toll of Fashion — 7
5. Chapter 5: From Pollution to Solutions — 9
6. Chapter 6: The Power of Conscious Consumerism — 11
7. Chapter 7: The Role of Policy and Regulation — 13
8. Chapter 8: The Rise of Slow Fashion — 15
9. Chapter 9: Innovations in Sustainable Fashion — 17
10. Chapter 10: The Influence of Culture and Media — 19
11. Chapter 11: The Business Case for Sustainability — 21
12. Chapter 12: The Future of Fashion Retail — 23
13. Chapter 13: The Impact of Fashion on Climate Change — 25
14. Chapter 14: Ethical Fashion Brands Leading the Way — 27
15. Chapter 15: Fashion Activism and the Power of Community — 29
16. Chapter 16: Education and Awareness for the Future — 31
17. Chapter 17: A Vision for the Future — 33

1

Chapter 1: The Glitter and Gloom of Fast Fashion

The allure of fast fashion lies in its promise of trendy clothing at wallet-friendly prices. However, behind the glitzy facade is a murky reality riddled with ecological damage and unethical practices. For consumers, the joy of scoring the latest style often eclipses the grim truths about fast fashion's impact on the planet. From the excessive water usage in cotton production to the toxic dyes polluting water bodies, the ecological footprint of this industry is vast and troubling.

Beyond environmental issues, fast fashion frequently exploits labor in developing countries. Garment workers, many of whom are women and children, toil under harsh conditions for meager wages. This exploitation is woven into the fabric of the fast fashion supply chain, creating a cycle of poverty and disempowerment. Yet, the demand for cheap clothing persists, driven by the constant churn of trends and the allure of low prices.

Consumer behavior plays a crucial role in perpetuating this cycle. The phenomenon of "disposable fashion" encourages frequent purchases and rapid discarding, leading to an accumulation of textile waste. Landfills overflow with barely-worn garments, exacerbating the environmental crisis. Understanding this dynamic is the first step towards envisioning a more sustainable and ethical fashion industry.

The chapter concludes with a call to consciousness. As consumers, we wield significant power to influence change. By making informed choices and demanding transparency from brands, we can begin to unravel the harmful practices of fast fashion. The journey towards a sustainable future starts with awareness and collective action.

2

Chapter 2: The Hidden Cost of Cheap Clothes

The price tags on fast fashion items may be low, but the hidden costs are staggering. Every bargain tee or dress has a story of resource depletion and human suffering that seldom makes it to the storefront. Understanding these hidden costs requires delving into the supply chain, where the true price of cheap clothing is paid by the environment and vulnerable workers.

Water is one of the most heavily impacted resources. Cotton, a staple material in fast fashion, is a particularly thirsty crop. It takes approximately 2,700 liters of water to produce a single cotton t-shirt. The consequences are severe, especially in regions where water scarcity is already a pressing issue. The diversion of water for textile production can lead to the depletion of local water supplies, affecting both ecosystems and communities.

Chemical pollution is another significant cost. The dyes and treatments used to achieve vibrant colors and finishes often contain harmful substances. When these chemicals are discharged into rivers and streams, they contaminate water sources and harm aquatic life. The impact extends to human health, as people living near production facilities are exposed to toxic pollutants.

Labor exploitation is the human face of fast fashion's hidden costs. The race to produce ever-cheaper clothing leads to corners being cut on worker safety and wages. Factory disasters, such as the Rana Plaza collapse, highlight the extreme dangers faced by garment workers. Despite international attention and outrage, many factories continue to operate under unsafe conditions, prioritizing profits over human dignity.

This chapter emphasizes the importance of seeing beyond the price tag. Consumers need to recognize the true cost of their fashion choices and demand accountability from brands. Ethical consumption is not just about what we buy but also about how we value the lives and resources involved in production.

3

Chapter 3: The Environmental Footprint of Fast Fashion

Every piece of clothing has an environmental footprint that begins long before it reaches the store. The fast fashion industry's demand for rapid production and constant newness results in significant environmental degradation. From the extraction of raw materials to the disposal of finished garments, the ecological impact is profound and far-reaching.

Textile production is a major contributor to global carbon emissions. The energy-intensive processes involved in manufacturing and transporting clothing add to the industry's carbon footprint. Synthetic fibers, such as polyester, are derived from petroleum, linking fast fashion to fossil fuel consumption. The production and disposal of these fibers contribute to greenhouse gas emissions and plastic pollution.

Waste is another critical issue. Fast fashion's business model encourages frequent purchases and discards, leading to a massive amount of textile waste. It is estimated that over 80 billion pieces of clothing are produced annually, many of which end up in landfills within a year of purchase. The decomposition of synthetic fibers releases harmful chemicals into the soil and air, further exacerbating environmental harm.

Water pollution is a pervasive problem in textile production. The use of dyes, bleaches, and other chemicals results in toxic effluents being released into water bodies. These pollutants can cause severe ecological damage, affecting aquatic life and contaminating drinking water supplies. The lack of effective wastewater treatment in many production regions amplifies the problem.

The chapter concludes by highlighting the potential for change within the industry. Sustainable practices, such as using eco-friendly materials and reducing waste, can significantly mitigate the environmental footprint of fashion. Consumers can support this shift by choosing brands committed to sustainability and advocating for industry-wide reforms.

4

Chapter 4: The Human Toll of Fashion

Behind the glamour of fashion lies a stark reality for the millions of workers who produce our clothes. The human toll of fashion is borne by those laboring in sweatshops, enduring long hours, unsafe conditions, and insufficient wages. The drive for low-cost, high-volume production often comes at the expense of worker rights and dignity.

Garment workers are among the most vulnerable laborers in the global economy. Many are trapped in a cycle of poverty, unable to escape the exploitative conditions that characterize much of the industry. Wages are often below subsistence level, making it difficult for workers to afford basic necessities. This economic vulnerability is compounded by a lack of job security and benefits.

Unsafe working conditions are rampant in the fashion industry. Factory fires, building collapses, and hazardous environments are distressingly common. The 2013 Rana Plaza disaster, which resulted in the deaths of over 1,100 workers, is a tragic reminder of the dangers faced by garment workers. Despite international efforts to improve safety standards, many factories continue to operate without adequate protections.

Child labor is another dark aspect of the fashion industry. In some regions, children are employed in garment production, often performing arduous tasks for minimal pay. This exploitation deprives children of education and exposes them to health risks. The prevalence of child labor underscores the need for stringent enforcement of labor laws and ethical sourcing practices.

The chapter calls for a human-centered approach to fashion. Ensuring fair wages, safe working conditions, and respect for workers' rights should be fundamental principles of the industry. Consumers can play a role by supporting brands that prioritize ethical labor practices and demanding transparency in supply chains.

5

Chapter 5: From Pollution to Solutions

The environmental and human costs of fashion are daunting, but solutions are within reach. The shift towards sustainable and ethical fashion is gaining momentum, driven by consumer demand and innovative practices. Transforming the industry requires a collective effort from brands, consumers, and policymakers.

Sustainable materials are at the forefront of this transformation. Natural fibers such as organic cotton, hemp, and bamboo are being embraced for their lower environmental impact. Innovations in textile production, such as the development of bio-based and recycled fibers, offer promising alternatives to conventional materials. By reducing reliance on resource-intensive and polluting processes, these materials can help mitigate the industry's environmental footprint.

Circular fashion is another key solution. This approach emphasizes the reuse, recycling, and upcycling of garments to extend their lifecycle. Brands are adopting circular principles by designing products for durability and repairability, as well as implementing take-back and recycling programs. Consumers can contribute by choosing quality over quantity and embracing second-hand and vintage fashion.

Transparency and accountability are essential for driving change. Brands must be transparent about their supply chains and commit to ethical practices. Certifications and standards, such as Fair Trade and Global

Organic Textile Standard (GOTS), provide consumers with assurance of ethical and sustainable production. Policymakers can support these efforts by implementing regulations that promote environmental protection and labor rights.

The chapter concludes with a hopeful outlook. The fashion industry has the potential to be a force for positive change. By embracing sustainability and ethics, it can create a future where fashion is not only beautiful but also responsible. Consumers, brands, and policymakers all have a role to play in making this vision a reality.

6

Chapter 6: The Power of Conscious Consumerism

Conscious consumerism is a powerful force for change in the fashion industry. By making informed choices and prioritizing ethical and sustainable brands, consumers can drive demand for responsible fashion. This chapter explores the principles of conscious consumerism and how individuals can make a positive impact through their purchasing decisions.

Awareness is the first step towards conscious consumerism. Understanding the environmental and social implications of fashion choices empowers consumers to make informed decisions. Educating oneself about the issues, such as the environmental impact of textile production and labor exploitation, is crucial for becoming a responsible consumer.

Choosing quality over quantity is a fundamental principle of conscious consumerism. Investing in well-made, durable garments reduces the need for frequent replacements and minimizes textile waste. Consumers can look for brands that prioritize craftsmanship and offer warranties or repair services. Embracing a minimalist wardrobe and focusing on timeless, versatile pieces can also contribute to sustainable fashion consumption.

Supporting ethical and sustainable brands is another important aspect. Consumers can seek out brands that are transparent about their supply chains and committed to ethical practices. Certifications, such as Fair Trade and organic labels, provide assurance of responsible production. By choosing brands that prioritize sustainability and labor rights, consumers can support positive change within the industry.

The chapter encourages readers to take action. Conscious consumerism is not just about individual choices but also about collective advocacy. Supporting campaigns for industry reform, signing petitions, and engaging with brands on social media can amplify the call for ethical and sustainable fashion. The power of consumer voices can drive the industry towards a more responsible future.

7

Chapter 7: The Role of Policy and Regulation

Policy and regulation are essential in steering the fashion industry towards sustainable and ethical practices. Governments and international bodies have the power to enforce standards that protect both the environment and workers. This chapter examines the role of policy and regulation in creating a more responsible fashion industry.

Environmental regulations can significantly reduce the industry's ecological impact. Policies that limit the use of harmful chemicals, mandate sustainable sourcing of materials, and require proper waste management are critical. For example, the European Union's REACH regulation controls the use of hazardous substances in textiles, ensuring that products are safer for consumers and the environment.

Labor laws play a crucial role in protecting garment workers. Regulations that enforce fair wages, safe working conditions, and prohibit child labor are fundamental. The International Labour Organization (ILO) sets global standards for labor rights, but local governments must implement and enforce these standards effectively. Stronger labor laws can prevent exploitation and improve the quality of life for workers in the fashion supply chain.

Trade policies also influence the fashion industry. Tariffs, trade agreements, and import/export regulations can encourage or dissuade certain practices.

For instance, preferential trade agreements that reward countries adhering to environmental and labor standards can promote ethical production. Conversely, policies that ignore these standards can perpetuate harmful practices.

The chapter underscores the importance of advocacy and civic engagement. Citizens can influence policy by supporting campaigns for stronger regulations, participating in public consultations, and voting for leaders committed to sustainability and ethics. Collaborative efforts between governments, NGOs, and industry stakeholders are essential for driving meaningful change.

8

Chapter 8: The Rise of Slow Fashion

Slow fashion is a movement that challenges the fast fashion paradigm by emphasizing quality, sustainability, and ethical production. This chapter explores the principles of slow fashion and how it offers an alternative to the harmful practices of the mainstream fashion industry.

At its core, slow fashion prioritizes quality over quantity. Unlike fast fashion, which relies on mass production of low-cost garments, slow fashion focuses on creating timeless, durable pieces. This approach reduces waste and encourages consumers to invest in clothing that lasts. Slow fashion brands often use high-quality materials and craftsmanship, resulting in garments that can be worn for years.

Sustainability is a key principle of slow fashion. Brands in this movement prioritize eco-friendly materials, ethical sourcing, and minimal waste. For example, using organic cotton, recycled fibers, and natural dyes can significantly reduce the environmental footprint of clothing. Slow fashion also embraces local production, which supports local economies and reduces the carbon footprint associated with transportation.

Ethical production is another cornerstone of slow fashion. Brands committed to this movement ensure fair wages, safe working conditions, and respect for workers' rights. Transparency is essential, with many slow fashion brands providing detailed information about their supply chains. By fostering a direct relationship with consumers, slow fashion brands build trust and accountability.

The chapter concludes with practical tips for embracing slow fashion. Consumers can start by curating a capsule wardrobe, focusing on versatile pieces that can be mixed and matched. Supporting independent designers, buying second-hand, and learning to repair and upcycle clothing are other ways to adopt slow fashion principles. Ultimately, slow fashion is about making mindful choices that align with values of sustainability and ethics.

9

Chapter 9: Innovations in Sustainable Fashion

Innovation is driving the future of sustainable fashion. From groundbreaking materials to new business models, the industry is evolving towards a more responsible and eco-friendly future. This chapter explores some of the most exciting innovations in sustainable fashion.

One of the most promising areas of innovation is in materials. Researchers are developing bio-based and biodegradable fibers that offer a sustainable alternative to conventional textiles. For instance, fabrics made from algae, mushrooms, and fruit waste are gaining attention for their environmental benefits. These materials are not only renewable but also often require fewer resources to produce.

Recycling and upcycling technologies are also advancing. Innovative processes are being developed to recycle old garments into new fibers, reducing the need for virgin materials. Upcycling, which involves transforming waste materials into new products, is becoming more popular among designers and consumers. These practices help close the loop in the fashion industry, promoting a circular economy.

Technology is playing a significant role in sustainable fashion. Digital tools such as 3D printing, virtual fitting rooms, and blockchain are revolutionizing the way fashion is produced and consumed. 3D printing allows for on-demand production, reducing waste and excess inventory. Virtual fitting rooms enable consumers to try on clothes digitally, reducing the need for returns and exchanges. Blockchain technology enhances supply chain transparency, allowing consumers to trace the origins of their garments and verify ethical practices.

The chapter highlights the role of collaboration in driving innovation. Partnerships between researchers, designers, brands, and consumers are essential for advancing sustainable fashion. By sharing knowledge and resources, stakeholders can develop and implement solutions that benefit the environment and society. The future of fashion is one of creativity, innovation, and responsibility.

10

Chapter 10: The Influence of Culture and Media

Culture and media have a profound influence on fashion. They shape consumer perceptions, trends, and values, playing a crucial role in the shift towards sustainable and ethical fashion. This chapter examines how culture and media can drive positive change in the fashion industry.

Fashion is a reflection of cultural values and societal norms. As awareness of environmental and social issues grows, there is a corresponding shift in cultural attitudes towards fashion. Movements such as minimalism, eco-consciousness, and ethical consumption are gaining traction, influencing consumer behavior and preferences. Cultural leaders, including celebrities, influencers, and activists, play a significant role in promoting sustainable fashion.

Media is a powerful tool for raising awareness and educating consumers about the impact of their fashion choices. Documentaries, articles, and social media campaigns highlight the issues within the fashion industry and showcase sustainable alternatives. Platforms like Instagram and YouTube provide a space for advocates and influencers to share information and inspire change. By amplifying the voices of sustainable fashion advocates, media can drive demand for responsible fashion.

Storytelling is an effective way to engage consumers and create an emotional connection to sustainable fashion. Brands that share their journey towards sustainability, highlight the artisans behind their products, and communicate their values can build loyal customer bases. Authentic storytelling fosters transparency and trust, encouraging consumers to support ethical and sustainable brands.

The chapter encourages readers to engage with culture and media critically. By seeking out diverse perspectives and staying informed about the latest developments in sustainable fashion, consumers can make more conscious choices. Engaging with brands on social media, supporting campaigns for change, and sharing information within their communities are ways to contribute to the cultural shift towards sustainable fashion.

11

Chapter 11: The Business Case for Sustainability

Sustainability is not just an ethical imperative; it also makes good business sense. Companies that embrace sustainable practices can benefit from increased customer loyalty, operational efficiencies, and long-term profitability. This chapter explores the business case for sustainability in the fashion industry.

Consumer demand for sustainable fashion is growing. As awareness of environmental and social issues rises, more consumers are seeking out ethical and eco-friendly brands. Companies that prioritize sustainability can tap into this demand, gaining a competitive edge in the market. Brands that are transparent about their practices and committed to continuous improvement build trust and loyalty among consumers.

Operational efficiencies are another benefit of sustainability. Sustainable practices, such as reducing waste, conserving resources, and optimizing supply chains, can lead to cost savings. For example, energy-efficient production processes and water-saving technologies can lower operating costs. By minimizing waste and maximizing resource use, companies can improve their bottom line while reducing their environmental impact.

Risk management is a critical consideration for businesses. Companies that ignore sustainability face increasing regulatory, reputational, and financial risks. Regulatory requirements for environmental and labor standards are becoming stricter, and companies that fail to comply may face fines and legal action. Reputational risks, such as negative media coverage and consumer boycotts, can damage a brand's image and profitability. By proactively addressing sustainability, companies can mitigate these risks and enhance their resilience.

The chapter concludes with a discussion of long-term profitability. Sustainable practices can contribute to a company's long-term success by fostering innovation, attracting investment, and building brand equity. Investors are increasingly prioritizing environmental, social, and governance (ESG) criteria when making investment decisions. Companies that demonstrate a commitment to sustainability can attract investment and access capital for growth. By integrating sustainability into their core business strategy, fashion brands can create value for both shareholders and society.

12

Chapter 12: The Future of Fashion Retail

The retail landscape is evolving, driven by changing consumer preferences and technological advancements. The future of fashion retail is one that prioritizes sustainability, transparency, and customer experience. This chapter explores the trends and innovations shaping the future of fashion retail.

Omnichannel retailing is becoming the norm. Consumers expect a seamless shopping experience across online and offline channels. Retailers are investing in technologies that integrate their digital and physical presence, providing a consistent and personalized experience. For example, augmented reality (AR) and virtual reality (VR) technologies enable consumers to visualize how garments will look and fit, enhancing the online shopping experience.

Sustainable retail practices are gaining prominence. Retailers are adopting eco-friendly store designs, using renewable energy, and implementing recycling and waste reduction programs. Pop-up shops and temporary retail spaces are being used to reduce the environmental impact of permanent stores. By creating spaces that reflect their commitment to sustainability, retailers can attract eco-conscious consumers and differentiate themselves in the market.

Transparency and traceability are essential for building trust with consumers. Retailers are using technologies such as blockchain to provide detailed information about the origins and journey of garments. This transparency allows consumers to make informed choices and ensures accountability within the supply chain. Retailers that prioritize transparency can build stronger relationships with their customers and enhance their brand reputation.

Customer experience is at the heart of future retail strategies. Personalization, convenience, and engagement are key drivers of customer satisfaction. Retailers are using data analytics and artificial intelligence to personalize recommendations, offer tailored promotions, and optimize inventory management. Interactive and immersive shopping experiences, such as in-store events, workshops, and virtual reality try-ons, are transforming the way consumers interact with brands.

The rise of direct-to-consumer (DTC) brands is reshaping the retail landscape. These brands bypass traditional retail channels and sell directly to consumers, often through online platforms. This model allows for greater control over branding, pricing, and customer experience. DTC brands are known for their agility and ability to quickly respond to consumer demands, making them well-suited to the fast-paced fashion industry.

Sustainable packaging is becoming a priority for retailers. The fashion industry generates a significant amount of packaging waste, much of which ends up in landfills. Retailers are exploring eco-friendly packaging options, such as biodegradable materials, reusable bags, and minimalistic designs. By reducing the environmental impact of packaging, retailers can align with consumer values and contribute to a more sustainable industry.

The chapter concludes with a vision for the future of fashion retail. As technology continues to evolve, retailers will need to adapt and innovate to meet the changing expectations of consumers. By prioritizing sustainability, transparency, and customer experience, the fashion industry can create a retail environment that is both responsible and engaging.

13

Chapter 13: The Impact of Fashion on Climate Change

Fashion is not just a matter of personal style; it has a significant impact on the planet's climate. The industry's carbon footprint is substantial, contributing to global greenhouse gas emissions and exacerbating climate change. This chapter explores the relationship between fashion and climate change and highlights the steps needed to mitigate the industry's impact.

The production of textiles, especially synthetic fibers like polyester, is energy-intensive and relies heavily on fossil fuels. The extraction, processing, and transportation of raw materials contribute to the industry's carbon emissions. Additionally, the energy consumption of factories and the global logistics network adds to the environmental burden. The fashion industry is responsible for approximately 10% of global carbon emissions, making it one of the most polluting sectors.

The use of unsustainable practices, such as overproduction and waste, further exacerbates the industry's impact on climate change. Fast fashion's business model encourages frequent purchases and disposals, leading to an excessive amount of textile waste. Landfills overflowing with discarded garments release methane, a potent greenhouse gas, as they decompose. Incineration of textile waste also releases harmful emissions, contributing to air pollution and climate change.

Water usage is another critical issue. The fashion industry is one of the largest consumers of water, with cotton production alone accounting for a significant portion. The irrigation of cotton fields depletes water resources, particularly in regions already facing water scarcity. The contamination of water bodies with chemicals and dyes used in textile production further compounds the environmental impact.

The chapter concludes with a call to action. Mitigating the fashion industry's impact on climate change requires a concerted effort from brands, consumers, and policymakers. Brands can adopt sustainable practices, such as using renewable energy, reducing waste, and sourcing eco-friendly materials. Consumers can make conscious choices by supporting sustainable brands and reducing their consumption. Policymakers can implement regulations that promote environmental protection and incentivize sustainable practices.

14

Chapter 14: Ethical Fashion Brands Leading the Way

In the quest for a more sustainable and ethical fashion industry, certain brands stand out as pioneers. These companies are leading the way with innovative practices, transparent supply chains, and a commitment to environmental and social responsibility. This chapter highlights some of the ethical fashion brands making a difference.

Patagonia is a trailblazer in sustainable fashion. Known for its commitment to environmental stewardship, the brand uses recycled materials, advocates for fair labor practices, and donates a portion of its profits to environmental causes. Patagonia's "Worn Wear" program encourages consumers to buy used gear, repair their clothing, and recycle garments at the end of their life cycle.

Stella McCartney is another influential figure in the ethical fashion movement. The designer's eponymous brand is known for its cruelty-free and sustainable practices. Stella McCartney uses innovative materials, such as vegan leather and recycled polyester, and maintains a transparent supply chain. The brand's commitment to sustainability extends to its retail spaces, which feature eco-friendly designs and renewable energy.

Everlane is celebrated for its "radical transparency" approach. The brand discloses the true cost of its products, including materials, labor, and transportation, and provides detailed information about its factories.

Everlane's commitment to ethical production and fair wages sets a high standard for transparency in the fashion industry.

The chapter concludes by emphasizing the importance of supporting ethical fashion brands. By choosing to buy from companies that prioritize sustainability and ethics, consumers can drive demand for responsible fashion. The success of these brands demonstrates that it is possible to create beautiful, high-quality clothing without compromising on values.

15

Chapter 15: Fashion Activism and the Power of Community

Fashion activism is a powerful force for change. Grassroots movements, advocacy groups, and passionate individuals are driving the conversation around sustainability and ethics in the fashion industry. This chapter explores the role of fashion activism and the power of community in creating a more responsible fashion landscape.

Fashion Revolution is a global movement that advocates for transparency, sustainability, and ethics in the fashion industry. Founded in response to the Rana Plaza disaster, Fashion Revolution encourages consumers to ask brands, "Who made my clothes?" Through campaigns, events, and educational resources, the movement raises awareness about the impact of fashion and empowers consumers to demand change.

The rise of social media has amplified the reach of fashion activism. Platforms like Instagram, Twitter, and TikTok provide a space for activists to share information, mobilize supporters, and hold brands accountable. Influencers and advocates use their platforms to highlight issues within the industry and promote sustainable alternatives. The power of social media lies in its ability to connect people across the globe, creating a collective voice for change.

Community initiatives, such as clothing swaps, repair cafes, and sustainable fashion markets, foster a sense of collaboration and shared responsibility. These events provide opportunities for individuals to engage with sustainable fashion practices, build relationships, and learn new skills. By participating in community initiatives, consumers can contribute to a culture of sustainability and reduce their environmental footprint.

The chapter concludes by encouraging readers to get involved in fashion activism. Whether through social media, community events, or supporting advocacy groups, individuals can make a meaningful impact. The collective power of community and activism is a driving force for a more ethical and sustainable fashion industry.

16

Chapter 16: Education and Awareness for the Future

Education is a critical component of the shift towards sustainable and ethical fashion. By raising awareness and providing the tools for informed decision-making, education can empower individuals to drive change. This chapter explores the role of education in shaping the future of fashion.

Integrating sustainability into fashion education is essential for cultivating a new generation of designers and industry professionals. Fashion schools and universities are increasingly incorporating sustainability into their curricula, teaching students about eco-friendly materials, ethical production practices, and circular design principles. These programs prepare students to lead the industry towards a more responsible future.

Public awareness campaigns play a vital role in educating consumers. Initiatives that highlight the environmental and social impact of fashion can change consumer behavior and drive demand for sustainable alternatives. Documentaries, articles, and social media campaigns provide accessible information and inspire action. By making sustainability a mainstream topic, public awareness campaigns can create a cultural shift towards responsible fashion.

Industry collaborations with educational institutions can also drive progress. Brands partnering with universities and research organizations can support the development of sustainable technologies and practices. These collaborations can result in innovative solutions that benefit both the industry and the environment. By investing in education and research, the fashion industry can foster a culture of continuous improvement and innovation.

The chapter concludes by emphasizing the importance of lifelong learning. Consumers, industry professionals, and policymakers must stay informed about the latest developments in sustainable fashion. Engaging with educational resources, participating in workshops, and staying up-to-date with industry news are ways to continue learning and contributing to positive change. Education is the foundation for a sustainable and ethical fashion future.

17

Chapter 17: A Vision for the Future

The journey towards a sustainable and ethical fashion industry is ongoing, but the progress made so far offers hope for the future. This chapter envisions a fashion industry that prioritizes environmental stewardship, social responsibility, and innovation. By embracing these principles, the industry can create a future where fashion is both beautiful and responsible.

In this vision, sustainability is integrated into every aspect of fashion. From design to production to disposal, every step of the process is guided by a commitment to minimize environmental impact. Sustainable materials, renewable energy, and circular design principles are standard practices. Brands are transparent about their supply chains and accountable for their actions.

Social responsibility is at the heart of this future fashion industry. Garment workers are treated with dignity and respect, earning fair wages and working in safe conditions. Child labor and exploitation are eradicated, and labor rights are upheld globally. The industry values the people behind the products, fostering a culture of fairness and equity.

Innovation drives the industry forward. Advances in technology, materials, and business models continually push the boundaries of what is possible. Brands, consumers, and policymakers work together to create innovative solutions that benefit both the industry and the planet. Collaboration and creativity are key to achieving a sustainable and ethical fashion future.

The chapter concludes with a call to action. The vision for a sustainable and ethical fashion industry requires collective effort and commitment. Consumers, brands, policymakers, and activists all have a role to play in making this vision a reality. By working together, we can create a future where fashion is a force for good, reflecting our values and protecting our planet.

From Fast Fashion to Forever: Ecology and Ethics in the Clothing Industry

In a world captivated by ever-changing trends and disposable fashion, **"From Fast Fashion to Forever"** delves deep into the hidden costs and consequences of the clothing industry. This thought-provoking book unravels the glittering facade of fast fashion, revealing the stark realities of its environmental footprint and human toll.

Through 17 insightful chapters, readers will journey through the heart of the fashion industry, exploring the exploitative labor practices, excessive resource consumption, and chemical pollution that underpin cheap, trendy clothing. The book offers a comprehensive examination of the industry's impact on climate change, highlighting the urgent need for sustainable and ethical alternatives.

Amidst the grim realities, the book shines a light on hope and innovation. Discover the rise of slow fashion, the power of conscious consumerism, and the role of policy and regulation in driving change. With stories of ethical fashion brands leading the way and the growing influence of fashion activism, this book inspires readers to envision a future where fashion is both beautiful and responsible.

"From Fast Fashion to Forever" is not just a critique but a call to action. It empowers consumers to make informed choices, advocates for stronger regulations, and celebrates the innovators and activists paving the way for a sustainable and ethical fashion industry. Whether you're a fashion enthusiast, an eco-warrior, or simply curious about the clothes you wear, this book provides the knowledge and inspiration to transform the way we think about fashion.

www.ingramcontent.com/pod-product-compliance
Lightning Source LLC
LaVergne TN
LVHW020458080526
838202LV00057B/6017